A TROOP OF THE GUARD

AND OTHER POEMS

A TROOP OF THE GUARD

AND OTHER POEMS

BY

HERMANN HAGEDORN

BOSTON AND NEW YORK
HOUGHTON MIFFLIN COMPANY
MDCCCCIX

TO THE MEMORY OF MY MOTHER

LOFTY IN THOUGHT, GENEROUS IN SERVICE
BRAVE IN TROUBLE
AND EVER PATIENT, LOVING, WISE
I DEDICATE
WHATEVER IN THESE VERSES
IS WORTHY OF HER DEAR
AND GENTLE SPIRIT

CONTENTS

THRENODY: A. H. 1849–1909   xi

PART I

LINCOLN: AN ODE   3
A TROOP OF THE GUARD: HARVARD CLASS
    POEM   10
LINES ON MEMORIAL DAY   15
THE MIGHTIER POESY   19

PART II

SONG   27
THE WORSHIPERS   28
REBELS   29
SONG AT MIDNIGHT   30
SONG IN DARKNESS   31
A PARTING   32
FORGIVENESS   39
LINES TO A DOG   40
"WHERE E'ER MY WAYS GO"   42

TO A LARK OF THEBES   43

THE GLORIOUS BONDAGE   44

THE AWAKENING   46

RETURN   47

SONGS FROM THE ROCKIES

    I. "INTO THE WILDERNESS, COME!"   50

    II. REVEILLE   50

    III. "DID YOU SEE ME COMING, LOVE?"   51

    IV. THE LEAVEN OF TWILIGHT   51

    V. DAY'S END   52

    VI. NIGHT RIDE   53

PART III

MIDNIGHT IN EUROPE, TWILIGHT IN
NEW YORK   57

BATTLE SONG OF THE HOPEFUL   63

FOG   64

FIGHTERS   65

SONG OF THE GRAIL SEEKERS   66

SUNDAY MORNING ON FIFTH AVENUE   67

CALM SEA   68

THE GREATER BIRTH   69

TO A BELOVED COMPANION   71

HYMN TO ARTEMIS   73

" MY TRUE LOVE FROM HER PILLOW ROSE "   74

AUTUMN TWILIGHT   75

SONG UNDER THE STARS   76

WINTER   77

APPREHENSION   78

RESIGNATION   79

THE GARDENS OF FERRARA   80

ODE BY THE SEA   84

SONNET IN CANDLELIGHT   87

CONCERNING SONNETS   88

SUMMER'S END   89

SONG FROM THE GARDENER'S LODGE   90

SONG OF THE WICKED FRIAR   92

LULLABY   93

PART IV

FIVE IN THE MORNING: 97

     A DRAMATIC POEM IN ONE ACT

The author extends his thanks to the editors of the following maga-
zines for permission to reprint the subjoined poems : *The Atlantic Monthly*,
" My True Love from her Pillow Rose " ; *The Forum*, " Midnight in
Europe, Twilight in New York," and " Song from the Gardener's
Lodge."

THRENODY

A. H.

1849–1909

I

How gently broods the Sabbath o'er the earth !
  The fervid west wind, driving o'er the sea
His champing stallions, hums with quiet mirth,

Not pain, as yestermorn ; not misery
  As yesternight, whose pallid child, the moon,
In heaven's gold chamber where the slow days die,

Sobbed in her silver cradle. Soon, too soon,
  She sank to rest, but lo, the sea, the wind,
Sing with new voices and the bent reeds croon.

The frail, white child with outstretched arms is kind.
  The mists that harrowed like far crowded ships
The sea's marge, flee before her, and the blind

And stumbling sun breaks from his dark eclipse
  Of storm, and grants, with largess never guessed,

Silk for the sea's robe, jewels for her breast,
Peace to her spirit, music to her lips.

II

Oh, glowing day of rapture and soft airs!
  How often have thy kindred, glad as thou,
Played at my side and sped my childish cares,

Lightly! Alas, thou canst not speed them now —
  The tears that burn unshed within my eyes,
The heaviness that weighs upon my brow!

I gaze on thy large bounty and surmise
  That hearts somewhere may leap at thy glad call;
But to my sight in strange and spectral guise

Thou comest — like a shadow leading all
  Thy far dead shadowy brothers in thy train —
Those dear lost days in which a sparrow's fall

Was tragedy, a finger-prick was pain,
  And love was as the sky without a cloud,
A deep, felicitous, unplumbed domain.

Oh, sweet, far days! The voices that were loud
  In your brief reign are hushed. That dearest
        voice —
That knew not to be bitter, nay, nor proud,

Nor aught that was not pure and of God's choice—
    Silence hath borne it to his own far hill
As he bears all earth's music, to rejoice

Alone over his treasure. Mute and chill
    I watch the pageant of mankind surge by.
She is not there! And can I linger still

Toiling and planning, laughing even as I
    Laughed, as she sat beside me and laughed,
        too?
How strangely we live on when loved ones die!

I wander down the solemn beach, and through
    The long dune grass, and in my heart the pain
Of dreaming of those other days with you,

My mother, whom I shall not see again,
    Clutches me, till the looming form of Death,
Towering above me with his large disdain,

Makes all that is, a bubble and a breath.
    I listen to the sea, the dismal sound
Of surge and ebb, that like a crying wraith

Moans to the sand its pain till pain is drowned
    In louder-tongued despair. Grief like a storm,
A passion, a wild hope, forever bound

To unavailing longing, her chill form
  Presses against my breast. Oh, pale, pale face,
So cold and silent where my joy was warm

With converse and clasped hands and love and
      grace!
  Oh, spectral shape, that like a mist I feel
Drawing all things into thy wide embrace!—

I know that not for man is joy or weal
  More than a flitting hour, but oh, dark bride—
  Of men and ghosts and dreams and love and
      pride,
Art thou the only comrade that art real?

                        III
Oh, fragile house of joy, melodious
  And sunny chambers, of what airy stuff
Are built your walls, that the imperious

And single word of death should be enough
  To shatter them forever? We are men
Racing upon the sharp and perilous bluff

That overhangs despair. Beyond our ken,
  The reason of our striving and its goal
Lie undiscerned. One wins a crown, and ten

Into the mute and dismal blackness roll
    Where walk the sorrowful, and none may guess
How soon the shades shall close above his soul.

Out of the deep a thousand questions press.
    Unanswering, we plod on, unknowing, strive;
    For at our heels the sweeping ages drive,
And we must toil and toil and acquiesce.

IV

Upon the silent shore alone with grief
    I sat and pondered on the lost, dead years.
How ardent the desires, how pale, how brief,

Fulfillment; how of dust and of the spheres
    Compounded is man's love, and lo, how soon
In the deep, ever-brimming cup of tears

Melts the bright pearl that is God's greatest
        boon!
    Love, what art thou that we should cry to thee
As the waves cry unto the silent moon?

Thine end is loneliness and misery,
    The yearning of the sleepless for the day,
    A frail remembrance, at whose feet we lay
Our poor, dumb gifts of pain and constancy!

What is thy consolation, O my God,
  To us who mourn? Not cheap forgetfulness,
That 'neath the living blanket of green sod

Love's long devotion and her deep distress
    Would bury. Nay, nor other loves, more young,
More joyous, with pure hands and lips, to dress

The heart's wound till it heal. Such hands have clung
  Compassionately to mine, such lips have given
The tender pity of a strong soul, wrung

With kindred anguish, but man's deep heart riven
  Of death finds not its comfort thus, nor peace.
Each love has its own tears, nor earth nor heaven

Can with fresh gifts of glory bid men cease
    Mourning the lost. Sweet friend, not you nor I
Can from the other's bleeding heart release

The crushing hands of sorrow. Though the cry
  Of our desire be one, and of our love,
    Our faith, our ultimate hope — beside us move
Still our twain griefs that cannot blend nor die.

VI

The day turns dusk. Through the light sand I plod
  Homeward, and ponder on my fruitless woe.
What is thy consolation, O my God?

I watch the creamy ripples surge, and flow
  Back to the heart of waters. This dark sea,
This is eternal. Ages come and go

O'er its proud surface, sadly, laughingly,
  Bringing their storms, their wailings, their calm
    sleep.
But never death, nor silence! What if we

Should on a wide and spiritual deep
  Be the pale waves that from the azure bourn
An instant greet the earth's light, laugh and weep

Beneath the sun, and happily return
  To the embracing Unity? Ah, then
'T is not for us to sit apart and mourn

For those who from the shallow sight of men
  Have sunk back to that sea! For we are one —
The living and the dead — I, denizen

An instant of this earth, you who have gone,
  My mother, still beside me, though unseen!
Then let the cries of my despair be done!

I cannot lose that which hath ever been
  And ever shall be! You are here, my true,
Clear-sighted friend! No space can intervene

With mortal barriers now 'twixt me and you!
  I need not speak, for ever must you hear
Th' unspoken love; nor cry, nor yet renew

The pleading of my anguish, for your ear
  Is tuned to music subtler than man's thought.
Lo, as I stand beneath the stars, and peer

Over the pale-ridged sea, the dusk hath brought
  Your presence to my spirit's new-born sight.
You stand beside me, silent, where I sought

Only my grief. I feel the old delight
  Of comradeship, I see your deep, blue eyes —
With joyful tears after long parting, bright,

As oft they were — so pure, so steadfast, wise,
  I feel my soul as from a cloudy vale
Light and exultant as a skylark rise!

I do not fear what Death, the strong, the pale,
  Surging upon life's beaches, may destroy.
  With open hands I yield earth's temporal joy;
The mightier rapture Death cannot assail.

xviii

PART I

LINCOLN: AN ODE

LET silence sink upon the hills and vales!
  Over the towns where smoke and clangor tell
Their glad and sorrowfully noble tales
    Of women bent with care, of men who labor
      well,
Let silence sink and peace and rest from toil.
  Oh, vast machines, be still! Oh, hurrying men,
Eddying like chaff upon the frothy moil
Of seething waters, rest! In tower and den,
High in the heavens, deep in the cavernous ground,
There where men's hearts like pulsing engines bound,
Let silence lull with loving hands the sound.

Silence — ah, through the silence, clear and strong,
Surging like wind-driven breakers, sweeps a song!
  Out of the North, loud from storm-beaten strings,
Out of the East, with strife-born ardor loud,
Out of the West, youthful and glad and proud,
    The cry of honor, honor, honor! rings.

(Read at the Lincoln Centenary Celebration of the Military Order of
the Loyal Legion of the United States, Commandery of Pennsylvania,
at the Academy of Music in Philadelphia, February 12, 1909.)

And clear with trembling mouth,
Sipping in dreams the bitter cup, the South
    Magnanimous unfeignèd tribute brings.

Oh, prosperous millions, hush your grateful cries!
    The sanctity of things not of this earth
        Broods on this place —
Wide things and essences that have their birth
In the unwalled, unmeasured homes of space;
Spirits of men that went and left no trace,
    Only their labor to attest their worth
In the world's tear-dim, unforgetting eyes:
    Spirits of heroes! Hark!
    Through the shadow-mists, the dark,
Hear the tramp, tramp, tramp of marchers, living,
        who were cold and stark!
    Hear the bugle, hear the fife!
        How they scorn the grave!
    Oh, on earth is love and life
        For the noble, for the brave.
        And it 's tread, tread, tread!
    From the camp-fires of the dead,
Oh, they 're marching, they are marching with their
        Captain at their head!
    Greet them who have gone before!
    Spread with rose and bay the floor —
They have come, oh, they have come, back once
        more!

4

Give for the soldier the cheer,
For the messmate the welcoming call,
But for him, the noblest of all,
Silence and reverence here.
Oh, patient eyes, oh, bleeding, mangled heart!
 Oh, hero, whose wide soul, defying chains,
  Swept at each army's head,
  Swept to the charge and bled,
Gathering in one too sorrow-laden heart
 All woes, all pains:
 The anguish of the trusted hope that wanes,
The soldier's wound, the lonely mourner's smart.
He knew the noisy horror of the fight.
From dawn to dusk and through the hideous night
 He heard the hiss of bullets, the shrill scream
  Of the wide-arching shell,
 Scattering at Gettysburg or by Potomac's stream,
Like summer showers, the pattering rain of death;
With every breath,
 He tasted battle and in every dream,
  Trailing like mists from gaping walls of hell,
  He heard the thud of heroes as they fell.
Oh, man of many sorrows, 't was your blood
 That flowed at Chickamauga, at Bull Run,
Vicksburg, Antietam and the gory wood
And Wilderness of ravenous Deaths that stood
Round Richmond like a ghostly garrison:
 Your blood for those who won,

For those who lost, your tears!
For you the strife, the fears,
For us, the sun!
For you the lashing winds and the beating rain in
your eyes,
For us the ascending stars and the wide, unbounded
skies.

Oh, man of storms! Patient and kingly soul!
Oh, wise physician of a wasted land!
A nation felt upon its heart your hand,
And lo, your hand hath made the shattered whole.
With iron clasp your hand hath held the wheel
Of the lurching ship, on tempest waves, no keel
Hath ever sailed.
A grim smile held your lips while strong men
quailed.
You strove alone with chaos and prevailed;
You felt the grinding shock and did not reel.
And, ah, your hand that cut the battle's path
Wide with the devastating plague of wrath,
Your bleeding hand, gentle with pity yet,
Did not forget
To bless, to succor, and to heal.

Great brother to the lofty and the low,
Our tears, our tears give tribute! A dark throng,
With fetters of hereditary wrong

6

Chained, serf-like, in the choking dust of woe,
Lifts up its arms to you, lifts up its cries!
Oh, you, who knew all anguish, in whose eyes,
    Pity, with tear-stained face,
Kept her long vigil o'er the severed lands
    For friend and foe, for race and race;
You, to whom all were brothers, by the strands
    Of spirit, of divinity,
        Bound not to color, church, or sod,
        Only to man, only to God;
You, to whom all beneath the sun
    Moved to one hope, one destiny —
    Lover of liberty, oh, make us free!
Lover of union, Master, make us one!

Master of men and of your own great heart,
    We stand to reverence, we cannot praise.
    About our upward-straining orbs, the haze
Of earthly things, the strife, the mart,
    Rises and dims the far-flung gaze.
    We cannot praise!
We are too much of earth, our teeming minds,
Made master of the beaten seas and of the con-
        quered winds,
    Master of mists and the subservient air,
Too sure, too earthly wise,
Have mocked the soul within that asks a nobler prize,
    And hushed her prayer.

We know the earth, we know the starry skies,
And many gods and strange philosophies;
    But you, because you opened like a gate
    Your soul to God, and knew not pride nor hate,
Only the Voice of voices whispering low ——
You, oh my Master, you we cannot know.

    Oh, splendid crystal, in whose depths the light
    Of God refracted healed the hearts of men,
        Teach us your power!
        For all your labor is a withered flower
    Thirsting for sunbeams in a murky den,
Unless a voice shatters as once the night,
    Crying, Emancipation! yet again.
For we are slaves to petty, temporal things,
    Whipped with the cords of prejudice, and bound
Each to his race, his creeds, his kings,
    Each to his plot of sterile ground,
    His narrow-margined daily round.
Man is at war with man and race with race.
We gaze into the brother's face
    And never see the crouching, hungry pain.
    Only the clanking of the slavish chain
We hear, that holds us to our place.

    Oh, to be free, oh, to be one!
    Shoulder to shoulder to strive and to dare!
    What matter the race if the labor be done,

What matter the color if God be there?
Forward together, onward to the goal!
Oh, mighty Chief, who in your own great soul,
  Hung with the fetters of a lowly birth,
  The kinship of the visionless, the obstinate touch
    of earth,
Broke from the tethering slavery, and stood
Unbound, translucent, glorious before God! —
Be with us, Master! These unseeing eyes
  Waken to light, our erring, groping hands
    Unfetter for a world's great needs!
  Till, like Creation's dawning, golden through the
    lands
Leaping, and up th' unlit, unconquered skies
    Surging with myriad steeds,
There shall arise
Out of the maze of clashing destinies,
  Out of the servitude of race and blood,
  One flag, one law, one hope, one brotherhood.

A TROOP OF THE GUARD

HARVARD CLASS POEM

THERE's trampling of hoofs in the busy street,
  There's clanking of sabres on floor and stair,
There's sound of restless, hurrying feet,
Of voices that whisper, of lips that entreat,
    Will they live, will they die, will they strive, will
      they dare?
The houses are garlanded, flags flutter gay,
For a Troop of the Guard rides forth to-day.

Oh, the troopers will ride and their hearts will
      leap,
    When it's shoulder to shoulder and friend to
      friend —
But it's some to the pinnacle, some to the deep,
And some in the glow of their strength to sleep,
    And for all it's a fight to the tale's far end.
And it's each to his goal, nor turn nor sway,
When the Troop of the Guard rides forth to-day.

(Read before the Graduating Class of Harvard College, June 21, 1907.)

The dawn is upon us, the pale light speeds
  To the zenith with glamour and golden dart.
On, up! Boot and saddle! Give spurs to your
    steeds!
There's a city beleaguered that cries for men's deeds,
  With the pain of the world in its cavernous heart.
    Ours be the triumph! Humanity calls!
      Life's not a dream in the clover!
    On to the walls, on to the walls,
      On to the walls, and over!

    The wine is spent, the tale is spun,
    The revelry of youth is done.
    The horses prance, the bridles clink,
    While maidens fair in bright array
    With us the last sweet goblet drink,
    Then bid us " Mount and ride away ! "
    Into the dawn, we ride, we ride,
    Fellow and fellow, side by side;
    Galloping over the field and hill,
    Over the marshland, stalwart still;
    Into the forest's shadowy hush,
    Where spectres walk in sunless day,
    And in dark pools and branch and bush
    The treacherous will-o'-the-wisp lights play.
    Out of the wood 'neath the risen sun,
    Weary we gallop, one and one,
    To a richer hope and a stronger foe

And a hotter fight in the fields below —
Each man his own slave, each his lord,
For the golden spurs and the victor's sword!

Friends of the great, the high, the perilous years,
Upon the brink of mighty things we stand —
Of golden harvests and of silver tears,
And griefs and pleasures that like grains of sand
Gleam in the hour-glass, yield their place, and die.
Like a dark sea our lives before us lie,
And we, like divers o'er a pearl-strewn deep,
Stand yet an instant in the warm, young sun,
Plunge, and are gone,
And over pearl and diver the restless breakers sweep.
On to the quest! To-day
In joyful revelry we still may play
With the last golden phantoms of dead years;
Hearing above the stir
The old protecting music in our ears
Of fluttering pinions and the voice of her,
The Mighty Mother, watching o'er her sons.
To-day we still may crouch beneath her wings,
Dreaming of unimagined things;
To-morrow we are part
Of the world's depthless, palpitating heart,
One with the living, striving millions
Whose lives beat out the ceaseless, rhythmic song
Of joy and pain and peace and love and wrong.

We may not dwell on solitary heights.
There is a force that draws men breast to breast
In the hot swirl of never-ending fights,
When man — enriched, despoiled, oppressed,
By the great titans of the earth who hold
The nations in their hands as boys a swallow's nest —
Leaps from the sodden mass through loves and feuds
And tumult of hot strife and tempest blast,
Until he stands, free of the depths at last,
A titan in his turn, to mould
The pliable clay of the world's multitudes.

An anxious generation sends us forth
On the far conquest of the thrones of might.
From West and East, from South and North,
Earth's children, weary-eyed with too much light,
Cry from their dream-forsaken vales of pain,
" Give us our gods, give us our gods again ! "
A lofty and relentless century,
Gazing with Argus eyes,
Has pierced the very inmost halls of faith,
And left no shelter whither man may flee
From the cold storms of night and lovelessness and
        death.
Old gods have fallen and the new must rise !
Out of the dust of doubt and broken creeds,
The sons of those who cast men's idols low
Must build up for a hungry people's needs

New gods, new hopes, new strength to toil and
    grow ;
Knowing that nought that ever lived can die,
No act, no dream but spreads its sails, sublime,
Sweeping across the visible seas of Time,
Into the treasure-haven of eternity.

The portals are open, the white road leads
    Through thicket and garden, o'er stone and sod.
On, up! Boot and saddle! Give spurs to your
    steeds!
There's a city beleaguered that cries for men's deeds,
    For the faith that is strength and the love that is
        God!
        On through the dawning! Humanity calls!
        Life's not a dream in the clover!
        On to the walls, on to the walls,
            On to the walls, and over!

LINES ON MEMORIAL DAY

I

Lift up your hearts, ye people, and be proud!
  Oh, mourn no more the fallen in the fray;
  Peace and a nation's glory wrap their clay,
And they sleep well who sleep in such a shroud.

II

Lift up your hearts, ye people, and be proud!
Not of the dead alone,
Above whose shattered frames the stone
Records the glory and the tears,
The triumph of tempestuous years —
Not of the dead alone, nation of men, be proud!
Out of the dust of those who fought and fell,
Out of the dreams of those who slumber well,
Thy mightier armies, firm, uncowed,
Up to thy fields of battle crowd.

III

Honor the dead!
Honor with garlands, honor with wreaths,
Honor with roses, white and red!

Honor, all else above,
Honor with love,
In whose depths still a nation's passion seethes.
Honor with songs the glories that have been!
But more, thrice more,
Honor with reverence the dreams,
The wingèd hopes that madly soar,
The failing glimpses, transitory gleams,
That from the watch-tower of a prophet's thought
Tell of the greater battles still unfought,
The greater glories still unseen.

IV

Not in the tale of stirring fights,
Not in the triumph song,
That tell of mighty days and nights
When right has conquered wrong;
Not in men's deeds doth glory rest!
Only in vision, pure and high,
Only in faith, in spotless zest
And dauntless hope doth glory lie.

V

Honor the past, but honor more the dreams,
Misty to-day, that are to-morrow's deeds —
Those momentary dim imaginings,
In whose swift fire the light of æons gleams
On dark, undreamt, gigantic things —

Telling strange tales of peoples and of kings,
Of growing labors, growing needs;
Of bloodless battles, frantic years
And Niobean tears;
Strange, sombre songs whose throbbing undertones
Are toiling women's cries, and strong men's groans.
They tell of new rebellions that shall come
When from the East, the West, the South, the North,
From Oregon, from Maine,
From Texas and the blazing plain,
Men shall go forth
Without the cheer of flag and drum
To fall as erst their fathers fell;
And o'er the graves no stone shall tell
The mighty cause; no wreath
Sweeten the slumbers of the dead beneath.

VI

Honor the living, honor the brave,
Honor the strong who daily fight
'Gainst hunger and a pauper's grave,
In crowded cities, on the perilous seas,
In reeking, clanging factories,
In mine-shafts, where
From murky dawn to dusking night
Herculean aliens, Goth and Hun,
Toil in the prisoned air
And never see the sun.

17

VII

Honor the great, self-risen, to rule the earth;
Honor the petty, who can be but tools;
Honor the drudges, bound to office stools;
Honor the mothers, pining at a hearth;
Honor the fallen, dauntless in their woes,
The mighty host who will not quail nor cry;
Let the dead sleep — and give your tears for those
Who, living, struggle and attain or die.

THE MIGHTIER POESY

THE din of crashing worlds is in the air.
Stars burst on stars, the hungry earth gapes wide,
Men die, things die, the monarch in his pride,
The slave at toil, the eager priest at prayer,
The poet crying challenge to the wind,
Challenge to chaos from undaunted lips —
They die, creeds die, dogmas and all that stood
Rock-strong through time, before a greater Flood,
A shock, a silence, and a dark eclipse,
Sink, and alone upon an unmarked strand
With burning eyes that dare not look behind,
The noble few survivors stand
To win with torch and spear an unknown mightier
   land.

One era dies, with fearful pangs the next,
Groping from chaos, feeble, doubting, young,
Lisping strange accents with untutored tongue
That falters still with wonder, half-perplext —
The new age rises from the hut, the den,
Rayed with new splendor, to the thrones of men.

(Read before the Signet Society of Harvard College, January 21, 1909.)

19

And with the age new gods, and with the gods
New creeds that soar on brave and untried wings,
New dreams that grapple with titanic things,
Circling with glory earth's still slumbering clods;

New tones, new voices! Hear them! They are loud
With monstrous sounds from wide, unpeopled tracts,
Loud with the roll of hundred cataracts
Bound in men's service, bound but yet uncowed!—

Loudest in cities!—in the din and roar
Of factory and traffic, in the chant
Of clashing steel on steel reverberant,
The shriek of whistles, rush of cars that pour

Their hurrying multitudes in turbulent streets —
Where, loud and clear, new tales of strife and gold,
New Iliads, new Odysseys unfold,
With voyages strange, strange triumphs, strange
        defeats.

New songs, new songs! I hear the void caves fill
With rolling chords and in tumultuous towns
I see the Muse that died with kings and crowns
Live in the blast-fires of an iron-mill!

I hear her in the air, I see her form
Riding the passionate whirlwind of great deeds,

Clangor about her and the rush of steeds
Sweeping mad riders on through night and storm,

Upward, upward! I see her in still places,
Where death and terror reign and life and love,
Where joy and anguish mark the upturned faces,
There, there, I see her move.

I see her in the citadels of trade
Where armies strive with armies; hot and long
The fight endures, while arms and hands grow faint,
Hearts that were strong
Falter before the fire, heads cringe beneath the blade,
And heroes without fear or taint
Lead on their soldiery from field to field
To win or lose, but never yield.
Among those fighters — struggling as of old
Trojan and Greek fought on the sandy plain,
Struggling with heart and brain,
Arms and their shield, a word;
Men of a sterner mould
Than ancient hosts who fought with javelin and
        sword —
There, by that sea whose curling waves are gold,
Do you not hear the Muse that bent to Homer's
        will
Crying that still strife lives, that men are heroes
        still?

I see her in the streets, where through long days
Besieging hosts clamor at brazen gates.
In terror-stricken rout
Nerve-racked as in a maze,
With timid heart and angry shout
Encamped they lie about the massive walls;
And through the days within the marble halls
The strong-willed moulders of men's little fates
Fight for their own hearths and their foes' the bat-
        tle with the wraith
Of panic in the cringing souls of men of little
        faith.

Ah, mighty Muse, again I hear thy song,
Again I feel hot in my heart thy measure, loud and
        strong,
Again I see thee — in the night
Wingèd above the place, where from the far
And steel-bound distances, with shrieking cries,
The dragons, many-limbed, with flaming eyes,
As on some conjurer's business, to and fro,
Through the great road-yard sweeping go.
Back from the funnel, star on golden star
Flings to the dusk its glamour; thick and white
The smoke-clouds roll.
And in the engine's brain
Where human hands hold in control
The splendid onward flight

Of this strong thing of steel and fire that half is god
      and soul,
The grimy firemen toil and sweat and strain,
Hour by hour
Holding undimmed the monster's power.
Do you not hear the Muse's fluttering wings
In the hot piston's throb, the whistle's wails,
The rumble and the thunderings
Of freighted cars on gleaming rails?
Lo, do you see her not by saving lights that gleam
From smoky bridges, turrets gray,
Marking of many ways, the way?
The signal lamps! The white and now the red
And now the white again! —
As strange and causeless-seeming as a dream!
Yet, oh, the mighty faith that to one human
      head,
Alert upon the central tower,
Gives o'er the lives of hundred thousand men!

I hear the factories throbbing, I see the furnace
      a-light,
Flaunting the new time's glory in the face of the
      welcoming night;
I see the hand of the master and loud from torrent
      and fen
I hear the moans of titans made slaves to the will
      of men.

23

Down to the dust the withered, up from the dust
the young!
Crying for hearts to uphold them, crying for sabre
and tongue;
Soldiers to right old wrongs,
Singers to sing new songs —
Songs that are half of the whirlwind and half of the
great calm's birth!
Songs of the brave, the wise,
Songs of the gold, the lies,
Songs of the Spirit of Man crushing the Spirit of
Earth!

PART II

SONG

Song is so old,
Love is so new —
Let me be still
And kneel to you.

Let me be still
And breathe no word,
Save what my warm blood
Sings unheard.

Let my warm blood
Sing low of you —
Song is so fair,
Love is so new!

THE WORSHIPERS

A SHRINE stood in the forest
  And we two knelt and prayed —
You to the kindly Master,
  I to the hill and glade.

Ah, humbly you prayed for the virtue
  God gave as a crown at your birth;
You pleaded for grace and the spirit —
  And I for the gifts of earth;

For the comforting arms of Nature,
  For the flash of a bird on the wing,
For the cold, white promise of winter
  And the warm fulfillment of spring;

For the whole great circle of marvels
  With me as a link in the chain!
You prayed to the king of your silence,
  And I to the wind and rain. —

Your hand touched mine and I held it,
  And the spirit cried low in the clod;
We kissed — and forgot our pleadings,
  And Nature and shrine and God.

REBELS

You and I and the hills!
  Do you think we could live for a day,
With the useless, wearying wrongs and ills
  And the cherished cares away?
Rebels of progress and our clay —
Do you think we could live for a day?

You and I and the dawn,
  With the great light breaking through,
And the woods astir with a wakened fawn,
  And our own hearts wakened, too;
With the bud in the hollow, the bird on the spray,
Do you think we could live for a day?

You and I and the dusk,
  With the first stars in the glow —
And the faith that our ills are but the husk
  With the kernel of life below;
With the joy of the hills and the throb of the May,
Do you think we could live for a day?

SONG AT MIDNIGHT

THE moon was so clear to-night,
  Who would have thought that the wind
Could draw such mists across the light,
  With the storms behind,
      To-night?

So strong was your heart, my sweet,
  Who would have thought that I
Had power to crush it under my feet,
  Nor heed your cry,
      My sweet?

SONG IN DARKNESS

Leave me not now, O love, leave me not now!
You that have wandered with me through the night,
Leave me not now!
In the deep valley lies the dawning light,
And on your brow
The shadows pale before our one great love —
Leave me not now!

Leave me not now, O love — the night is done;
The stars that watched so silently above
Our vale of trouble quiver from our sight.
Day has begun —
Ah, sweet, leave me not now!
Take not from me the pale, white joy upon your
            brow!
Love has not died, I know love has not died;
And must we watch, alone and weary-eyed,
For tumult and the night
To bring our souls together in our love?

A PARTING

LIKE watchers by the weary bed
Of one to whom death brings surcease
Of lingering anguish and for suffering peace —
When at the last the eyes, seeming to sleep, are dead —
We two watched pass the dying year.
The room wherein we sat was dimly lit and drear;
Only the grate gave out a glow
From ashes brown, vermilion-veined,
And half burnt coals that flickered low.
Before the paling fire we crouched,
Shoulder to shoulder, as of old
Beside the sea in happy idle Junes,
'Neath cloudless canopies of azure, couched
By sloping sands and overhanging dunes,
We watched the tumbled breakers that up the steep
      beach strained.
In the far town the church bells tolled,
And in the streets we knew that men were full of
      cheer,
Shouting and glad, crying to far and near:
" Happy New Year! "

She trembled. In my hand I took
Her hand, that unresisting shook.
" Happy New Year ! " we said,
Even though we knew that happiness was dead.
She turned to me. Her cheeks were stained
With tears she could not quite repel,
Though in her fair blue eyes a light,
Flashing as when the blue-winged pigeon turns
Wheeling in flight,
Told she had fought them well.
She spoke. " No more the glory burns,
The dream has waned.
Come, let us part ere all the glamour dies."
Her voice was low and strong ; I could not see her eyes,
For shadowed were my own. Like thief,
Or murderer condemned to lifelong prisonment
I gazed upon my handiwork, her grief,
And to her verdict nodded dumb consent.
" The dream has waned, yet it was fair," she said.
" There have been tears, but there was laughter once,
And care-free joy
As none on earth can find but only girl and boy,
Knowing not loss nor pain nor dread
On their oasis in the windy waste
Of the encircling fear-bent millions.
Now we must part. Good friend, do not rebel.
The splendor of the vision is effaced,
The halo of our fearlessness is gone.

Let us that knew the sun
Not be content in twilight dim to dwell.
We cannot blame each other nor our God.
The mocking, perilous world wherein secure we
    trod
Has at the first sign of our fainting hearts,
Our faltering feet, our wavering eyes,
Choked in its coils our paradise.
We should have trusted more in God and in each
    other.
Now all our weak attempts, our anxious arts
Are impotent before the doubts that chill and quench
    and smother."

She paused, and rising, stood
A while against the mantel, gazing deep
Into the ashes' crevices that glowed.
Upon her face I saw the womanhood
New-risen, stand —
A dismal conqueror of a wasted land,
Gazing from lofty summits o'er the sweep
Of hard-won kingdoms, counting high the cost
By which a host to victory rode,
Since all but pride was lost.
Her lips were pale, yet even now they smiled
As wearily she turned to me her face.
" Not by indifference our love shall be defiled,
Nor shall the heart's new tide erase

Before our eyes love's symbols on the sands.
To-morrow you must go."
And still she smiled, as though
To tell me that a day's quick smart
Would heal her heart.
I took in mine her hands.
A moment all the tumult of the days
When first we loved by the white stormy sea
Flamed up in me,
A mighty blaze,
That leaping from my lips encircled us
With fire that burned the world and burned the
        doubt, the pain,
And gave us all our love and all our faith again.
And for a flash I held her thus.
I cried : " Now are you mine at last!
The anger and the doubt are past,
The long uncertainty is done
And dead the sorrows, every one.
Together let us go our way —
With this new year shall life begin —
Together let us face the fray,
Together battle, strive and win.
Give me your lips, my sweet, my sweet!
Over the hills the clouds are fled — "
" True love is long, but passion fleet,
Nay, you must go," she faintly said.
Swift from my arms she fled away.

35

" To-morrow you must go — nay, it is late — to-day.
Go out to labor and to fight,
Both have we lessons hard to learn.
In the far years, return !
Blame not yourself nor me — the clock strikes one —
　　good-night."

The year's first morning all in splendor lay;
Cloudless the sky, frosty and clear the air
As though a god had swept the soiled world bare
Of last year's imperfections and decay.
Soft and untrammeled lay the snow.
Now must I go.
Into the clear white day we went.
The sleigh bells tinkled in the street;
Under our feet
The smooth snow crunched; and overhead
The sparkling branches, sighing, bent.
Of idle things we spoke —
How fair the elm, how straight the oak,
How blue the sky above the snow.
Yet ever, ever in each word
In every tinkling bell I heard
The chill refrain, " Now you must go."
Thus to the open road we came.
Behind, the village lay ; before,
The great world without end or aim,
Aged and dreamless, stark and hoar.

And then we parted; in the friendly press
Of hand in hand, the smile, the parting wave
Across the widening breach, what passer could
      have told
That here lay anguish and distress;
And in the smile's half-willed caress
Who would have dreamt the pain it gave?
I went, and drew my cloak close round me for the
      cold.

II

And now lies silence on the world
With all its joys in shadow furled.
The ringing song of life is hushed.
Out of the tumult of the street,
The cries of triumph, of defeat,
Out of the moan of spirits crushed,
Only the noisy wings of wrong
Flapping about men's hearts I hear,
Only the discord, shrill and clear,
Never, O God, the song.
Never the hope-filled heart leaps high,
The dreams untrammeled seek their goal —
Black, stricken shapes the visions lie
In my besiegèd soul.

Almighty God, let me not chide!
Not to my heart has glory been denied,

37

Not to my breast the breast nor to my lips the kiss.
These arms have held a universe enchained,
These wayward feet,
Now faltering above the dark abyss,
Have trod in splendor, young and sweet.
What though the dream, the golden dream, hath
     waned?
Life gave its best. Nay, God, I will not chide.
The world is open. Let me go
Into the world and run my race,
And though the heavy feet be slow,
Lord, let me gain my place.
What though, within, the early hopes lie broken?
Into the midst of life with eager heart,
Through joy a prophet, I depart,
For unto me the Lord hath spoken.

FORGIVENESS

FORGIVE me that I could not understand
  The peerless wonder and the magnitude
  Of thy great soul. Forgive me that imbued
  With all youth's confidence, I let the hand,
That held to mine as to a promised land,
  Droop and grow chill. I loved thee, yet I viewed
  With eager heart the phantoms that elude —
  Fame, life — forgive, I could not understand.
Thou wilt forgive the anguish and the tears,
  And worse than tears, the arid tearlessness,
  When Time turns round each grain of the shift-
      ing sand;
Thou wilt forgive the silent, empty years —
  Yet one thought from the waste will chafe no
      less;
  " In my dark hour — he did not understand."

LINES TO A DOG

TRUE of heart and black of hair,
Faithful were you, my Dagobert!
A friend to me when first I came
Unknown of face, unknown of name,
And entered in your lady's heart
With loving lips and poisoned dart.

I loved you for the small, white hands
That played amid your ebon strands.
I loved you for the face that bent
Unto your face in soft content
With murmured, " Ah, such love is rare
As that I hold, my Dagobert! "
You saw us erst beside the sea
When first her fair eyes looked on me.
The twilight dimmed, the calm sea's moan
Sang low in ceaseless monotone,
While you strove with the languid tide
And I with love and she with pride.

Old Dagobert, the seas will climb
Up those gray shores till end of time,

But you are dead, and she and I
Are parted as the land and sky.
Blind children! who, when passion's thirst
Is dry, and passion's bubbles burst,
Must beat at love's time-braided chain
And rend each silken bond in twain!
Oh, rare is friendship, yet how soon
We cast it from us, when the boon
Is less than all that dreams desire —
Soft warmth, but not a passion's fire.

Old Dagobert, your house is chill,
While mine hath warmth and friendship still,
But you at least have in your ears
The voice that soothed you through the years,
Her touch upon your poor, black head —
For me the voice, the hands are dead.

Man knows not where your house may be —
In dust or in Eternity? —
Man knows not, and you little care,
Yet — God be with you, Dagobert!

"WHERE E'ER MY WAYS GO"

WHERE e'er my ways go,
   Love, there are you —
In cloud and starry night
   And morning dew.

On the sea's horizon
   And windy space,
At the valley's end, always,
   Your face, your face!

In calm and tempest
   And morning dew,
Through death and forever,
   Love, there are you!

TO A LARK OF THEBES

Oh, lark upon the fallow fields,
What make you here so far from home,
'Mid temple, tomb, and obelisk —
What make you here ?

Dark grandeur lies upon the hills,
And darker silence 'neath their crest
Where ancient emperors lie mute —
What make you here ?

What care you for the ancient days,
The south's unchecked, impetuous glow ?
Yours is the quiet upland wood —
What make you here ?

We two are aliens far from home.
Oh, bird, could we but turn our flight
Back to our own unfamèd fields,
Back to our joy !

THE GLORIOUS BONDAGE

In vain I shake love's bondage free,
   In vain I speed from land to land,
A thousand tongues cry out to me
   From town and peak and desert sand:
" Ye two are fettered by a tie
That shall not rust and cannot die."

Of tenderest weaving are the threads,
   Bound round our hearts a thousand-fold,
Of common joys and hopes and dreads
   And apple-boughs and sunset-gold —
The memories that sob and cry
Against our hearts and will not die.

Forever is the sea a bond,
   Its every wave hath laugh and tear,
That bear me from to-day beyond
   The encircling world to yester-year.
And still the dune-wind moans and sighs
With memories, with memories.

The myriad voices of the spring,
   The summer's warm, exuberant mirth,

44

The creeping autumn-frosts that fling
    Their scarlet mantle o'er the earth,
Wild winter, bleak and riotous —
Are each a woven part of us.

Withal, shall still our hearts resist?
    What is there that we blindly fear?
About us darkly wreathes the mist,
    But, ah, beyond, the skies are clear!
Yea, in the Maker's infinite scroll
Our lives are woven, soul in soul.

THE AWAKENING

Out of the dark your face returns,
  Out of the night my hands aspire,
Up to the starry heaven burns
  Once more, once more, the old love's fire.

Out of the silence comes your voice
  With the old lost tones I loved so well,
And the buried songs of my heart rejoice
  At the kindred notes that rise and swell.

Give me your love again, give me all,
  Give me your heart's each throb and beat!
From the seats of the scornful, lo, I fall
  A subject, humbly at your feet.

I have gone, a vagabond o'er the earth,
  I have sought, I have searched on land and sea —
But, oh, the heart that gave love's birth,
  Is the heart that holds love's best for me.

RETURN

I DREAMT last night that I had crossed the seas;
And in a valley where the fresh earth sprang
In the year's youth with pale anemones,
And all the boughs,
Drunk with the new-pressed wine of life, stood
  flushed
In riotous carouse
Of blossom-time and May, I found your house.
With eager steps I went.
Strange was the place and hushed;
No bird sang in the boughs, no breeze the whole
  day long;
Yet in the very silence was a song.
"And here she dwells," said I, "and here I find
  content."
With eager steps I went
Through all the sweet, intoxicating lure of spring.
Never, ah never, was clay more kin to soul!
About me in the air was murmuring
Of new-born voices, at my feet the sod
Cried in its new strength, joyous with new mirth;
Between the blue sky and the green, green earth,

47

A white veil like a radiant aureole,
Born of the blossoms, hung, to man the sign
That even clay can be divine
And that the earth is God.
And so I came unto your gate.
Behind the curtained window, was it you
I saw an instant, as with beating heart elate
I sped your garden through?
I do not know, for I have felt your glance
In the still desert when the camel's tread
Grew languid with the heat, and in my eyes
Bright, blinding figures leaped in flaming dance
Like river-flies,
A dance of living dreams and dreams that long were
        dead.
Behind that window-pane,
Darkly and fleet,
Seen, to be lost again —
So was it in the desert and the heat.
Ah, but not now the sinking of the heart!
I stood within the door. Ah, not a jest
Of desert heat was this.
Lithe as of old your form, fair as of old your
        face! —
Only the room's width now to part —
You sped across the narrow space —
Was this a dream?
Once more I held you — breast to breast

48

A rapturous instant — and above the gleam
Of bloom and spring a mightier glory shone:
As our two hearts sang unison
And our shut lives sprang open in a kiss.

SONGS FROM THE ROCKIES

I

"INTO THE WILDERNESS, COME!"

INTO the wilderness, come!
Here where the wild bees hum.
  The aspen leaves quiver,
  Now darkly, now bright,
  The willow-dim river
  Sings loud with delight,
Birds are a-singing and voices are dumb —
Into the wilderness, come!

II

REVEILLE

The wild horse prances down the glen,
The cowbell tinkles, clucks the hen,
The mother-pig grunts to her ten:
    "Get up, you lazy fools!"

The sun upon the tent-roof glows
And still we sluggards doze and doze,
The rooster in the barnyard crows:
    "Get up, you lazy fools!"

50

III

"DID YOU SEE ME COMING, LOVE?"

Did you see me coming, love,
  Down the hills to you?
Bees were all a-humming, love,
  Starry lay the dew.

In the canyon's hushes
  Motion was there none,
Only in the bushes
  Mute the spider spun.

Song was in the branches,
  Gently oozed the sap,
Peaceful lay the ranches
  In the valley's lap.

Oh, my heart was drumming, love!
  If you only knew!
Did you see me coming, love,
  Down the hills to you?

IV

THE LEAVEN OF TWILIGHT

So ends a day's immortal story,
  At eve to God, returning, sent;
On every mountain-top is glory
  And every valley breathes content.

51

Now break the twinkling hosts of heaven,
  Like daffodils, the purple plain. —
What if the noon be grim ? The leaven
  Of day's sweet end is cure for pain.

Fear not ! Beneath the earth's mailed bosom
  A kindly heart throbs, baffling wrong;
That stirs the bough to rapturous blossom
  And lulls the tempest into song !

What though the failing visions cheat us,
  The stony highway halt our gait —
I know that nothing can defeat us
  If we but love and serve and wait.

V

DAY'S END

Now the day
  Slips away.
Through the valley see him go,
  Down the canyon, soft of tread,
Up the mountain, o'er the snow —
  Now he's gone and dead.
Whither hath he fled ?
  Who shall know ?
Stars shine in his stead
  And the new moon low.

Moon in mask and domino
　　Trundles to his western bed.
Midnight! Heigh-ho!
　　Snuff the light.
　　Love, good-night!

NIGHT RIDE

Home from the glen through the gathering night,
　　Home 'neath a purpling sky,
Home to our tent in the first star's light,
　　We ride, my sweetheart and I.

The shadows are long, the spruces are black,
　　The sage-brush is misty and gray —
And dreamy and dim are the hills at our back
　　In the last pink glow of the day.

There's a ford to cross where the stream runs
　　　　swift —
　　To stirrup and bridle it leaps!
Now up the sharp bank with a galloping lift
　　And into the canyon's deeps!

The wind's in the branches, the dark shadows glide!
　　Old Night is astir with his tricks;
And the aspens stand pale by the stream at your side
　　As an army of ghosts by the Styx.

53

Now the moon's pale eye o'er the mountain's peak
   Stares like a startled owl,
And wild on the wild slopes, gray and bleak,
   Answers the coyote's howl.

Ride, ride, oh my dearest! The night foes may
      throng
   And gibber enchantments from crevice and pine —
But hush that loud heart! Love is sure, love is
      strong.
   No spectres shall harm. You are mine, you are
      mine!

PART III

MIDNIGHT IN EUROPE, TWILIGHT
IN NEW YORK

The Old World sleeps.
Over the wall of sea, dusky and wild —
Where the great tempest sweeps
Untrammeled, as a god that leaps
Forward to kiss the laughing wave, his love —
The New World, like a sleepy child
Whose small diurnal round is run,
Turns, too, her fair face from the sun.

The Old World sleeps, and in the dome above
The midnight constellations gleam
Over the shadowy shores, over the silent stream.
The mighty river dumbly flows.
By friendly wharves, the vessels dark,
Save one dim spark
That high upon the masthead glows,
In spectral solitude repose.
The red-roofed thorps, 'neath linden-bough and oak,
Clustered like berries in their leafy cloak
Dim at the foot of some north-warding hill,
Sleep in a dreamless slumber and are still.

Over the breathing fields the wooded knolls
Kindly as some old nurse keep zealous guard.
No light nor sound — only at intervals
A fettered comet, many-starred,
That on its steely path through the still country rolls
With distant thunder and the whistle's calls.
The Old World sleeps.
Dim storied cities indolent
With dreams and placid self-content;
Where even Time her hasting wings
Folds, and with generous hand o'er spire and wall,
O'er crooked street and dingy court and empty
    manor-hall
Her sweetest gift, her veil of mystery flings;
Cities, where jarring progress creeps
And wise professors still prefer
Nodding o'er mouldy texts with two or three
Than in the outer world's unresting stir
To wring from multitudes an immortality:
Mute by their turgid streams the dreaming cities lie.
Scarcely the tired night-watch their vigil keep;
No voice, no step, disturbs their round,
Only a brawler lurching, homeward bound,
Then silence once again — the moon's pale light —
    and sleep.

But in gigantic capitals the night
Brings not the silence and the well-earned rest.

Garish above them hangs the light
Mirrored from thoroughfares and wide cafés
And dazzling signboards hanging in mid-air
That undulating blaze.
An indistinguishable hum
Of many voices fills the street,
Where the defiled,
The idle, painted, overdressed,
The innocent, the fond beguiled,
The Jew, the Gentile, on a level meet,
And prince and pauper's child,
In Night's delirium.

In restaurants the tired musicians play
Through the long night again and yet again
The numbing strain
Of some light waltz that has its day.
The women chatter as they go in pairs,
Or at the corners singly stand and watch
The endless press
Of petty clerks, of millionaires,
Of pallid youths whose tale is told at twenty,
Of idle lookers-on at life who gaze but never guess
That underneath the very wickedness
Is anguish, dread, and loneliness a-plenty;
That underneath the habit of desire
Lives something higher
Than passing cynic eyes may catch —

A gleam of God beneath the scars,
A flickering, aching longing for the stars.
Yet, once again the whirlpool drags the forms
Onward and downward to the crags and storms.

Midnight and dusk — the New World goes to
      rest.
Midnight is here, but over-seas the day
Still hangs upon her mother's breast
An instant while the sunbeams play
On churches' glimmering vanes,
And higher yet and higher
Burst to fire
Coppern and golden on the window-panes
Of slender buildings towering o'er the bay.
Even in the great metropolis, the May
Has entered now in girlish loveliness.
In the dark churchyard where the dead
Sleep undisturbed in the engirding press
Of titan warfare and the meaner stress
Of broods that daily battle for their bread —
The elms rise up out of the desert's core
And brightly clothe their naked boughs once more.
Over the graves the young grass springs,
The robins hop from mound to mound,
And now the twilight brings
An end to whir of feet and clanging traffic's sound.
From every portal streams the eager horde —

Old men and young, women as strong as they,
Courageous as the Amazons in fray,
Counting no man their lord;
But playing each and each her part:
Honor to them! for they are strong of heart.

Out of the gates, women and men and boys,
Homeward they go out of the battle's moil —
Vigorous, free, bred at their birth to toil,
Toil in their eyes, and in their ears the noise
Like a sweet music, of the city's life,
Stirring their youth to strife.

And now the mighty buildings sleep.
Like insects through the gorge - like streets, in
        clouds
To north, to east, to west the thousands sweep.
The river-boats are black with crowds.
See, how they dot the slanting bridge and pass
Into the lighted cabins, how they mass
On the wide decks, shoulder to shoulder stand
While the chains rattle and the quick gong sounds.
Out of the dock's great open jaws, the boat
Moves to the farther strand.
A city's population is afloat,
Passing at twilight from the narrow bounds
Of its captivity — but to go back
Upon the morrow to the wheel and rack.

Like ghosts that melt before the sun
The city's toilers, when the day
Nods to the night and work is done,
Into the twilight fade away.
The peopled towers and the populous streets
Deserted lie as though an age had passed
Since man had last
Marked them with triumphs and defeats.
Dark silence and the memory of woe
Hold concourse in that place, and chill and low
Run whispers of man's hunger and man's greed,
His sorry crowns, his bitter wounds that bleed,
And ghosts are there, huge shapes and things that
    move.
But not in street or by-street, not in the towers
    above
That one face undisfigured, the face of kindly love.

The Old World sleeps, and over-seas
The New World lays her tools aside.
Oh, weary souls, the day's large gates stand wide.
Night murmurs welcome, night the friendly-eyed,
Night shall appease!
Children of two worlds — rest at ease.

BATTLE SONG OF THE HOPEFUL

OUT of the dark where the dumb, the unguerdoned,
　Watch o'er their anguish and nurture their woe —
We who are hopeful, though never so burdened,
　Forward undaunted, unswerving we go!

We trust, oh, we trust! And the great sun's above
　　us!
　Not yet shall they have us, the poorhouse, the
　　grave.
For here at our sides there are true hearts that love
　　us,
　And the good Lord is kind to the joyous, the
　　brave.

Let the battle be grim and a thousand assail us —
　By the sun that hath led us, we still will defy!
Though the fight go against us, our hope shall not
　　fail us,
　Though we die in the striving, we'll laugh as we
　　die.

FOG

THE murky dark which fled in sullen flight
  Before the dim and ineffectual day,
  Loath to retreat yet daring not to stay,
Hath left her pallid sister, foe to light,
Fog, pale oblivion, on the world. The blight
  Hangs over land and sea. The joyous spray
  Leaps and is lost, and in its cap of gray
The earth like some dark wizard slips from sight.

Now am I all alone with bending reeds,
  Soft sands, the clash of waves in civil strife,
    The yearning tide, the damp and salty air.
This hour are they mine — and all earth's needs,
  That strain like spent waves up the shores of life,
    Stretch out pale arms and whisper to me there.

FIGHTERS

FEARLESS, to rise or fall,
  Arm pressed to arm we stand —
Fighters are one and all —
  Brother, your hand!

Hark, to the rushing storm,
  Battle and windy night!
Here's to a sturdy arm,
  Here's to a winning fight!

Hail! Be it crown or pall,
  Triumph or wasted land —
Fighters are one and all —
  Brother, your hand!

SONG OF THE GRAIL SEEKERS

On, on, on, with never a doubt nor a turning,
We ride, we ride!
On, on, on, striving and aching and learning,
We ride, we ride!
With ever the light on our brows, in our hearts the
unquenchable yearning,
And the grail afar
Like a golden star
Burning and burning and burning!
We ride!

SUNDAY MORNING ON FIFTH AVENUE

I saw the Sabbath Day procession go
　　Down the long avenue, and in the crowd
　　I saw wan faces, shoulders weak and bowed,
　　Satiate eyes, and cheeks with painted glow,
Feigning a glory they can never know,
　　Robed in a splendor that is half a shroud.
　　I saw strong men, weary and pale and proud,
　　Crowned all with flaunting vanity and show —
Clay, clay triumphant! Ah, the mockery!
　　That strong men should have dreamt their dreams
　　　　for these,
　　That heroes should have died to make these free!
Not so! Our dreams clay shall not crucify,
　　Nor choke their strength in golden robes of ease!
　　Though clay be mighty, God's flame cannot die!

CALM SEA

How like a glowing woman lies the sea,
  Breathing beneath the stars! So calm, so still,
  So self-surrendering, without woe or will,
As one who knows the joys that are to be
And dreaming basks in her security.
  The moonlight is her girdle, starry-pearled;
  The silver surf that breaks about the world
Her gown's hem, rustling softly, ceaselessly.

Soon from the west will come the wind, her lover,
  Singing afar, Make ready, I am here!
And she will laugh and fling her arms above her,
  And her great breast will heave; and strong and
    clear
Will sound his voice, half earthly, half divine:
Love of the world, belovéd, you are mine!

THE GREATER BIRTH

I LEFT the crowded streets behind
    And down the straight white road I went,
To open field and wood and sky
    And weary-limbed content.

Dumb was the forest, dumb the glade,
    Still as a church the arching boughs,
Though low winds tossed my tumbled hair
    And played about my brows.

I slept, I woke. The sun was mine,
    The sky, the birds, the fields my own!
And I was neither man nor god —
    Nature was I, alone.

The springs of earth coursed in my veins,
    From head to heart, from hill to sea;
The trees were my stalwart sons, the flowers —
    My daughters that played on the lea.

The sky was my dear love, bending down;
    And I sang to her softly, I sang to her loud —

And, ah, my voice was the voice of the wind
  That chases the sea-born cloud.

I felt the heart-throbs of the world
  Beating in me the greater birth ;
And I sang, I laughed, I cried in my glee
  That I was part of earth !

Yet though the sunshine glistened fair,
  And clear springs sparkled in the sod,
I trembled as I raised my eyes,
  For I was part of God.

TO A BELOVED COMPANION

Sweet sister I have never known,
  Yet soul to soul I know so well,
Beyond the outward look, the tone,
  That mourning mother-love could tell!

Blue were your eyes, your cheeks were white
  As lilies in the morning dew —
'Tis so I see you in the night
  And whisper in my dreams to you.

On April's sunny breath you came,
  On chill December's winds you fled;
Nine years — yet not for me — the flame
  Burned among men and comforted.

The arms that clasped me, soft and warm,
  Still felt beneath their warmth the touch
Of your white, flower-wreathèd form,
  Your face, that they had loved so much.

The mother lips that smiled through tears,
  What did they whisper to us then —

71

To you, a star amid the spheres,
  To me, a new-born child of men?

I know not, yet I half divine,
  When night and tempest rack the soul,
'T is you who lay your hand in mine,
  'T is you who hold me to the goal;

And through the doubts, the chill dismay,
  The sin, the penance, and the rod,
'T is you who touch my lips and say,
  "Doubt not, doubt not, there *is* a God!"

HYMN TO ARTEMIS

Bow, my queen, unto your world!
  See, earth's tired children sleep:
All their little woes lie furled
  In the shadows, still and deep,
All their quiet tears are dry —
Sleeping all, save you and I.

Come, my queen, and bend your face
  To my face and hear my prayer!
I am weary of the race,
  Weary of the dragging care:
Take me to your silver breast,
Give me succor, give me rest.

Give me slumber, give me dreams,
  Give me power to fight again,
Lest the morrow's war that seems
  Hopeless, be not fought in vain.
Ay, for triumph, ay, for death —
Give me strength and give me faith.

"MY TRUE LOVE FROM HER PIL-
LOW ROSE"

My true love from her pillow rose
   And wandered down the summer lane.
She left her house to the wind's carouse,
   And her chamber wide to the rain.

She did not stop to don her coat,
   She did not stop to smooth her bed —
But out she went in glad content
   There where the bright path led.

She did not feel the beating storm,
   But fled like a sunbeam, white and frail,
To the sea, to the air, somewhere, somewhere —
   I have not found her trail.

AUTUMN TWILIGHT

Summer is dead, Summer is dead!
  From heavy branches drops the fruit,
The yellow fields are harvested
  And wan and destitute.

No more the wind sings in the stalks,
  No more the poppies seek the sun,
Back to his barns the reaper walks
  With Summer's labor done.

Hark! in the boughs the autumn air
  Rustles the torn and brittle leaves,
Murmurous, low, like the sleepy prayer
  Of a tired child that grieves.

SONG UNDER THE STARS

In the village are pleasure and music,
  Gay voices and twanging guitars —
But here in the brush there is only the hush
  Of night, and the chant of the stars;

The stars that sing low in the heavens
  Like children, returning at night
Down a dark forest stream, half asleep, half
    a-dream —
  So happy, so weary, so white.

WINTER

I GO, I go,
To the barren plains where the north winds blow,
　Where the branches snap in the teeth of the gale
And the march of the northern foe.
　To the empty hills and the frozen trail
　And the winds' low wail
　I go.

For Nature my Mother is old and chill
　And hath sore need of me.
Marvel of marvels, Church of God —
　Mother, I come to thee.

I come, I come,
Though the music of hill and plain be dumb,
　And the wind forget the rose it bore
In its wailings burdensome.
　Though the rose be dust on the temple floor,
　Through the shrouded door
　I come.

For Nature my Mother is old and chill
　And hath sore need of me.
Marvel of marvels, Church of God —
　Mother, I come to thee.

APPREHENSION

Upon a star in infinite space, alone
  I sit and watch the turning of the hours;
  About me lies the waste. No summer showers
  Sprinkle the dust with blossoms; sand and stone
Are the wind's harp, whose music is a moan
  As of some monster soul in doubt who cowers,
  Pale in the shade of heaven's eternal towers,
  Before that One whose strength makes weak his
    own.
Far, far away, the noisy sea of life
  Tosses and beats, dim as some melody
  Haunting the soul with half-remembered strains.
Through nightmare distances I watch the strife,
  And dumbly listen for that one dread cry
  That shall fling wide the Gate of Hundred Pains.

RESIGNATION

I KNOW that in the crowded town,
  I know that on the pleasant lea,
I know that on the silver down
  That meets the loud assailing sea,
Men sorrow, and the hot tears come.
Oh, aching heart, be dumb, be dumb!
  Thy woe is but a single leaf
  In the green garland of eternal grief.

THE GARDENS OF FERRARA

Oh, prince, my prince, be not so generous!
  The human heart is weak, it cannot bear
  As much of human kindness as of care!
Kill me! But crush my beaten heart not thus!
God! It was June and love encircled us,
  And June winds whispered in her wondrous hair.
Her cheeks were flushed; her throbbing breast, her
      eyes,
Held all of life and love and paradise!

Oh, prince, my prince, I could not bear to go
  From the deep silence of our templed isle,
  Where fields lay soft and glimmered, and the smile
Of heaven was ours, and breezes murmured low.
Beneath us sang the sea in ebb and flow,
  And in the cool of shadowed peristyle
And gardens dark in beauty riotous
The larks sang all their happiest songs to us.

Oh, prince, my prince, the summer days are spent —
  The fields are barren and the larks are fled;
  Within the wood the happy leaves lie dead,

80

And dead is love and surfeited content.
Let not your arm hold back its punishment!
   Mine were your house, your wine-cups and your
      bread,
Your heart — and in its silver depths, the prize —
Your sister of the songs and magic eyes.

Your sister — Prince! What is it that you name
   The love unbounded as the mighty sea?
   Is it the friendship that you bear to me
Or I to you bore, ere the bitter shame
Of treason and of perjured honor came?
   Is that the love which is so wide and free?
I loved — the dark sea closed above my form
And quenched my soul in cataracts of storm!

Ah, prince, my prince, you that are clear and pure
   As the pure sky on perfect summer days,
   That know not doubt's slow torture, nor the ways
That turn and turn and leave no soul secure,
How can you know the anguish we endure,
   We common thralls of human fame and praise,
That love but where love seems to flee from us
And scorn the love that is too generous?

I am a singer, builder I of dreams,
   Born to be tortured and to torture so
   The hearts of them that love me, and would know

The soul wherein the singer's beacon gleams.
Its light is bitterness, its liquid beams
    Leave wells of fire eternal where they flow;
Its look is grief, its touch is ended faith,
Its love is sorrow and its kiss is death.

Into your courts I came. You called me friend,
    Your sister —   Ah, well may your brows grow
        dark!
    Your sister loved as I, the field and lark,
Your sister loved my songs, and without end
Upon her lute her wondrous head would bend;
    Then, eyes uplifted, catch from mine the spark
That burned within the singer and the song,
And gazing thus, sing thus the whole day long.

Ah, June was on the world! God, what is man
    When June's warm, color-bound, luxuriant days
    Spread in a net of columbine, a maze
Of vistas, and from world to world the span
Of dreams unbroken is for nymph and Pan!
    What, then, are God's laws or men's human ways?
The larks sang in their covert — who shall blame
If to our open hearts God's glory came?

For love is God's own glory — low or high.
    Though deep the fault and stifling be the sin,
    Still is there place for breath of God within!

82

Still is there something reaching to the sky,
From out the torn breast and the broken cry,
    That knows that love to glory is akin!
That laws are human as the hearts they break,
And gods that give love cannot love forsake.

O princely giver of a thousand gifts,
    Let your hand slay me ere I see her face!
    Beyond death's door perchance a little space
And June shall come again, and God who sifts
The music from the silences, and lifts
    Perfection from the dust, may show us grace.
Fear you to strike? Let me then grasp the blade!
Death shall — she comes! Nay, I am not afraid!

ODE BY THE SEA

THE sea is calm before the low land wind.
　　The breakers' loud, imperious voices, stirred
As for a mighty cause, sink, and behind,
　　The black and awful ocean, charactered
In symbols of white wrath as by a hand,
　　Invisible, prophetic, now lies clean
　　As a washed slate. In azure and in green
　　　　It laughs to heaven — in purple and in gray —
While up the long dunes to the peopled land
　　　　Sound, like a love discarded, stalks away;
　　　　Only the trailing echoes of him stay
In garrulous ripples twittering to the sand.

Oh, beautiful and unperturbéd soul,
　　Divine, mysterious ! On thy billows sleeps
Music, and in the thunder of thy roll
　　Tempestuous prophecy, and in thy deeps —
As in a crypt where dim and silent ghosts
　　Walk, and are felt to pass, though never heard
　　Nor seen, but only terribly inferred —
　　　　Are all earth's sorrows, pettinesses, pains,
Laughter and tears and vaunting, childish boasts,
　　　　Muttering in those far and dark domains

84

Their secrets, till the listening hurricanes
Fling them like seaweed up the shaggy coasts.

Inscrutable epitome of life,
  Living, immortal! In thy heart is all
Man ever dreamed, or in his love, at strife
  With law, desired, though earth and heaven fall
Crashing about him! Triumph on thy wave
  Marches like Tamburlaine; war, with the beat
  Of myriad drums and strong, unfaltering feet,
    Cannons and musketry and men's loud cries,
Thunders reiterate; from cliff and cave
    Despair with black and inexpressive eyes
    Shrieks, and from ebbing seas that agonize
On rock-strewn shores, regret and hunger rave.

I know thy heart. Pain is its sombre lord
  As pain is lord of all who strive on earth.
A little while joy gleams, as on a sword
  The sunlight laughs, or on thy deep, the mirth
Of summer zephyrs, 'neath a calm white moon,
  Robes thy dark limbs in jewel-flecked brocade
  An hour as for a merry masquerade.
    How thy low combers laugh in dwarfish glee!
The world is malachite and silver; soon
    Storm, like a pirate looming silently
    Out of the mist, shall take thy gems in fee —
And where young Rapture sang, old Grief shall croon.

85

Grief is thine other self, twin soul and mate!
  Lone spirit, through thy shadowy palaces
Wandering like Niobe, intemperate
  Of tears, that are love's last, supreme caress.
She sings, and in the harsh surf beating high
  Up the brown sands, I hear the wailing dirge.
  Through the long night the melancholy surge
    Of ebbing waters like a dying prayer
Haunts me, and when the day with laughing eye
    Wakes the dull east, I seek thy strand, and there,
    Bowing her silvery, disheveled hair
O'er the world's feet, I see Grief, sobbing, lie.

Great brother of ourselves, in whose veins seethe
  Our passions and our anguish! Day by day
I stand upon thy shores. I see thee breathe
  Softly, as when a child grown tired at play
Sleeps with his toys; I see thee moan and fret,
  And all humanity, with press and noise
  Of its brief day, with agonies and joys
    Never half comprehended, from the deep
Rises and tells its glory, its regret.
    Dumbly I watch the pitiless breakers sweep,
    Crashing ashore, the souls that laugh, that weep.
I hear their voices. I shall not forget.

SONNET IN CANDLELIGHT

Now on my shoulder droops thy little head
  Resigned to weariness at last, to sleep.
  Mute are the rebel wailings, calm and deep
The bosom's gentle motion, comforted
Of every pain! How swiftly are they fled
  The day's loud cares! Above thee now I keep
  The shepherd's watch beside the weary sheep.
Slumber, dear lamb! No wolf shall near thy bed!

Over thy face I bend, thy little hands.
  And as I gaze, lo, all the mighty schemes
    That reason builds, triumphant over faith,
    Melt as the wave's crest in the sea, a wraith.
  And all man's wisdom is the light that streams
Glorious, where He who blessed the children stands.

CONCERNING SONNETS

A LITTLE sonnet is a dangerous thing!
   Born of the luring moon, and eyes impearled
With glance of eyes, that set a soul to sing
   In fourteen lines its secret to the world.
Love's secrets are but vain when lovers start
   To lay their offerings in the sonnet's mould;
And fourteen lines can bare the fullest heart
   Of every woe and rapture it can hold!
Yea, sonnet-singing is a treacherous pit.
   For though we cast a treasure down each day
To fill the chasm, yet no man hath wit
   To close that gap, till death shall show the way.
A sonnet is a pitfall and a snare —
Lover and poet, hear it, and beware!

SUMMER'S END

Now is the gray, the grievous season here,
  When from the east, on ponderous ashen wings,
  Storm, with his drab, importunate underlings,
Comes like a bailiff to the bankrupt year.
Now like a prodigal, with mock and jeer
  Driven from his threshold, while the sharp air
      stings
  His Lydian softness, clad in threadbare things,
Summer to prison totters, fallen and sear.

Now is the time when to the aching heart
  The ancient griefs, th' eternal questions rise.
  Man comes and goes, the glory in his eyes
Fades and is quenched; like brittle leaves depart
  All things that eye can see and hand secure:
  The laws of Life and Change alone endure.

SONG FROM THE GARDENER'S LODGE

WEE, pretty jewels have I three,
Frolicking under the chestnut tree.

Two are my diamonds, one my pearl —
Those are my boys and this my girl.

My oldest shall be a sergeant tall
With a walk and a beard like a general;

And an arm for his king and a heart for a wench,
And an itch in his bones to stick the French.

My second shall learn the ways of peace,
Of spreading bloom and field's increase,

Of spade and hoe and clod and seed,
Of dropping fruit and clinging weed.

Little he'll reck of war or fame —
But every bud he'll call by name.

Oh, and the youngest, oh, my pride,
'T is she will stay at her mother's side,

With broom and kettle and rag and pan
Till the good Lord send her a gardener-man;

And a lodge and children two or three
Frolicking under a chestnut tree.

SONG OF THE WICKED FRIAR

LAUGHING maiden, pretty maiden,
   With your eyes of brown —
Give me but a single look,
   I 'll wear it as a crown !

Give me but a kiss, my lass,
   And touch of hands so fair —
By faith, I 'll lay me down and die,
   Without a priest or prayer.

For Heaven is all too cool for love,
   And many good souls, I own,
Would rather tend the coals in pairs,
   Than play with pearls alone.

LULLABY

FOR M. O. H.

THE wind is humming lullabies,
　　The birds carol, happy and long,
The sea has forgot her stormy cries
　　And drones an old, old song.

And it's all for you, my bud of the Spring!
　　But, oh, when your sleepy lids fall,
The little white stars in the sky shall sing
　　The loveliest song of them all.

PART IV

"Five in the Morning" was one of four one-act plays presented by the Harvard Dramatic Club in Boston and Cambridge on the evenings of May 17, 18, and 20, 1909.   The cast was as follows : —

BROUGHTON	Mr. Robert M. Middlemas
BLAIR	Mr. James A. Eccles
SPRAGUE	Mr. Karl I. Bennett
GALLISON	Mr. Philip G. Clapp

FIVE IN THE MORNING

A DRAMATIC POEM

PERSONS IN THE PLAY

BROUGHTON . . . . *A Writer*
BLAIR ⎫
SPRAGUE ⎬ . . . . *Dry-goods Clerks*
GALLISON ⎭

*SCENE : Blair's room on the top floor of a cheap board-
ing-house on West Twelfth Street, New York.
The hall-door is on the right ; on the left is an-
other door leading to an adjoining room. The
only window is in the centre of the back wall.
It is open, and through it may be dimly seen
the outlines of roofs and chimneys, and a church
steeple not far distant. The first light of dawn
is in the sky. In the room, however, the single
gas-jet of the chandelier suspended from the ceil-*

97

ing is still burning. Only the essentials of furniture are there : a narrow bed to the left of the window, a bureau to the right; a washstand, of cheap wood and water-stained, against the left wall, forward; and a square kitchen table with three chairs a little to the right and forward of the centre of the room. A threadbare carpet is on the floor. The walls are plastered white with many cracks ; the only pictures on them are a stained engraving of St. Michael subduing the Dragon that hangs over the bed, and an etching in a soiled white frame over the hall-door. The time is four o'clock of a morning in late summer.

When the scene opens, Broughton is discovered in the centre of the stage, back, sitting on the floor by the window, gazing out over the city. He is about forty, with dark heavy hair and beard touched with gray. His face is thoughtful and deeply marked, his figure, when he stands up, is seen to be tall and strong. His dress is simple and inconspicuous ; his slouch hat lies on the floor beside him. He is smoking a pipe and blowing rings into the air, absolutely oblivious of the noise coming from the table where Blair, Sprague, and Gallison are playing poker. Blair is the youngest of the four, in the middle twenties. On his face, too, lie the marks

98

of struggle, without the calm of achievement that distinguishes Broughton. He wears what are known as "business clothes" — a brown sack-suit, turn-over collar, and brown tie. His companions, on the other hand, are distinctly overdressed, wearing collars that are too high, waistcoats and cravats that are too gaudy. Their appearance is decidedly "sporty." Sprague's face has that smoothness, his eyes that inscruta-bility, which are always suspicious. Gallison is Irish, with reddish hair and mustache and hu-morous eyes. Sprague and Gallison are in their shirt sleeves, about which they wear rubber arm-bands. Sprague's cuffs are stacked beside him, doing office as an ash-tray. All three men are smoking heavily.

As the Curtain rises boisterous laughter is heard. Sprague, seated at the right side of the table, is laughing convulsively, pounding the table and rocking backward and forward. Gallison, opposite him, sits tilted back in his chair, his thumbs in the armholes of his waistcoat, chuckling quietly as he balances himself. Blair, facing the audience, is fingering his cards nervously. His eyes are flashing with anger, his brows drawn together, his lips compressed.

99

Sprague

*(Controlling his mirth, sings breathlessly in a
cracked voice)*

Lucy had a little lamb
Little lamb, little lamb —

Gallison

(In a deep voice, taking up the song)

Lucy had a little lamb
Whose fleece was white as snow.

Sprague

(After another burst of hilarity)

And everywhere that Lucy went —

Blair

*(To Sprague, with an effort to control his feel-
ings)*

Well, when you're ready, play the game.

Gallison

*(Speaking with a brogue, a broad grin on his
face)*

Begad !
Don't ye feel squelched at y'ur untimely mirth,
Old Sprague, me boy ? It 's serious he is.
A moral man is Blair.

Sprague

Oh, God, he's moral!

A chorus-girl in tights'll make him faint —

Gallison

Particularly if her name was Lucy.

Blair

Well, are you through?

Sprague

He ain't so awful good.

Now I've heard say —

Gallison

(*In mock astonishment*)

Blair? It's a libel, sure.

Sprague

Now you don't know. These precious innocents —

Gallison

Ye don't say, Sprague! So wicked and so young!

Blair

(*Hotly*)

Now play the game, or quit!

Gallison

         Come, Sprague, me boy.
It's losing that he is. He wants to play.
They say that girls use up a heap of money —

Sprague

    (*Picking up his cards and exchanging three*)
And he so young. It's these poor, innocent youths —
      (*The clock in the church steeple outside strikes
        four*)

Blair

    (*Flinging his cards on the table and jumping up*)
I've had enough.

      (*He pulls a small roll of bills and some change
        from his trousers pocket, and throws them on
        the table. Throughout this scene his attitude
        is bitter and defiant*)

         There, that's not all I've lost.
It's all I've got, though, and you'll have to wait
Until I earn the rest at better business
Than this.

Gallison

    (*Counting the money and putting it with an
      expression of work-well-done in his pocket*)
    Oh, we can wait, me boy —

Blair

We, we!
You're a fine team to come at dead of night
To make me play off at a poker game
The debts I've tried to pay by honest means.
Well, you've got something out of me, at least.
Now move!

Gallison

Sure, if you want. It's late enough.

Sprague
(*Hooking on his cuffs leisurely*)
You haven't told us yet about the girl.

Blair
(*Restraining himself with difficulty*)
Get out, Sprague!

Broughton
(*Rising from his crouching position by the win-
dow and knocking the ashes from his pipe*)
Blair, I guess it's time for me.
You're looking tired. You need some sleep.

Blair

Just wait.

Broughton

You 'd better sleep. You lost ?

Blair

Oh, nothing much.

Gallison

Lose at the cards, ye know, ye win at love.

Blair

(*Clutching Gallison violently by the collar*)

Get out, now ! I 'll not promise that I 'll stand
Much more from you.

Gallison

Leave go ! Come, Spraguey boy.
The bull is mighty wild at mating time.

(*Blair makes a dart for him, but Gallison throws
open the door right and escapes. Sprague
follows, stopping in the doorway*)

Sprague

Broughton, we 'll wait for you. I 've got a story
That beats the best I 've ever told you yet.
Gallison split a —

Broughton

No, you need n't wait.

104

Sprague

Oh, we don't mind.   (*Exit*)

Blair

God ! How I hate that tribe !

Broughton

I did n't think to find them here. I hoped
To have an old-time midnight talk with you.
I 'm sick, Blair.

Blair

Sick ?

Broughton

At heart. I just returned
Last night from Maine. Things have gone precious
wrong —

Blair

(*With a quick indrawing of the breath*)
Then you 've found out ?

Broughton

Oh, so you know it, too ?
They kept things quiet, so I scarcely thought
You 'd heard. She   disappeared   on   Wednesday
night. —
Vane thinks she drowned herself. I can't think that.

Lucy was plucky. But she's gone. That's all.
I've known her since her cradle days, and now —
Well — now I've got to find her.

Blair

She is dead,

Vane thinks?

Broughton
I can't believe it.

Blair

Was she happy?

Broughton
I do not know. I meant to write to you
To call on her. You know she liked you, Blair,
That time I brought you round. I always hoped
Somehow that you might hit it off together,
And once I wrote her —

Blair

Wrote? About me, Broughton?

Broughton
(*Continuing, with a faint smile*)
Giving a lightning sketch of all your virtues.
I'm not a great success, I fear, as matchmaker.

106

Blair

(*Nodding, half bitterly*)

No — no — you 're not a great success.

Broughton

You 're tired.
I 've bothered you too much with my affairs.
You don't look well.

Blair

(*Bitterly*)

Would you, if day by day
You drudged at work you hated ?

Broughton

Can't I help you —

Blair

Broughton, you can't.

Broughton

Why, it 's the first time, then.
You used to come to me —

Blair

I won't come now !
No, you 're the last one in the world I 'd come to.

Broughton

Blair, that 's unkind.

107

Blair

I can't explain. Please go.
Don't think too harshly of me when I've gone.

Broughton

(*Looking up sharply*)

You're going away ? That's rather sudden.

Blair

Yes.

I've struggled in the shadow long enough.
I'm going somehow, somewhere, to the sunlight —
If there is any sunlight.

Broughton

(*Laying his hand affectionately on Blair's shoulder*)

Boy, head up !

Blair

(*Painfully*)

Broughton, don't look at me that way. It hurts.

Broughton

When do you go ?

Blair

This morning.

108

Broughton

                    I suppose
You don't mind telling where?

Blair
(*After a pause*)
                    I'd rather not.
Broughton
(*Humorously, but a trifle uneasily, nevertheless*)
You have n't robbed a bank?

Blair
                    No, there you 're safe.
But, Broughton, what I *might* do like a plague
Torments me night and day. I fear myself,
Broughton! Ten years of poisoning drudgery
Have dulled my senses, wizened up my soul,
Corroded all that once was bright within me,
Till I can feel the noose about my throat
Already, for the crimes I might commit.

Broughton
Come, Blair, you 're overworked. Sit down. We 'll
      talk.
Blair
(*Quickly and nervously*)
No, Broughton, no! Go now, if you 're my friend.

It's you that stirs the devils in me so!
I can't explain, I can't!
> (*Sprague suddenly appears at the door right,
> a cigarette in his mouth, which he does not
> remove as he calls familiarly to Brough-
> ton*)

Sprague
Coming, old man?

Broughton
(*Coldly*)

Don't wait for me, Sprague.

Sprague
Oh, I'll wait all right.
I guess you'll want to hear what I've to tell.
Something about a friend of yours.

Blair
(*Under his breath*)

What's that?

Broughton
All right, I'll come.

Blair
(*After a moment, slowly*)

Broughton, I wish — you'd stay.

Broughton

(*Looking at him sharply*)

Good-by, Blair. Bon voyage!

Sprague

So long, old man.

(*They go out. Blair watches the door, motion-less and in silence a while, misery and fore-boding on his face. Then suddenly he turns and crosses the stage quickly to the door on the left, where he halts, his hand on the knob*)

Blair

(*Calling in a low voice*)

Lucy! (*A pause*) If she can sleep, why stir her now God! If she knew that Broughton had been here!

(*His hand falls to his side. He lifts his head, suddenly, becoming aware for the first time of a faint smell of gas in the room. He sniffs the air, then turns to the middle of the room where the jet is still burning, strikes a match, and standing on a chair tries to discover the leak in the pipe. The match goes out, he lights another, but does not find the leak; then throws both matches in a corner and sinks into a chair by the table, pondering*)

111

What does Sprague know ? — A friend, he said, of
    Broughton's,
Something about a friend. That 's me — or Lucy —

    (*He gives a short, bitter laugh*)

Or both. If he should know — about it all ! —
Broughton would come and she would go with him,
Glad to be rid of one whom in a dream,
A nightmare, she had loved, but waking soon
Had gazed upon with eyes unveiled and cold,
Indifferent. — Indifferent ! The misery
That lies in that one word : Indifferent !

    (*A pause*)

And if Sprague knows — all, when will Broughton
    come ?
God ! Will he come before that clock strikes
    five?
" At five come to my door," she said — " at five.
No minute earlier. Then you may go
And take me to the utmost ends of earth
And I will vow never to hurt you more."

    (*He sobs suddenly, then pulling out his watch
       he lays it on the table before him and falls to
       studying it feverishly*)

If I can live till five ! That 's half an hour.
It might be easy then to live a day,
And other days. But oh, the drudgery ! —

Two piteous earthworms digging toward the light —
Scarcely we reached it, crushed beneath Fate's
heel.

> (*He goes to the window, snaps up the shade, and
> looks out*)

The same gray roofs, the same gray leaden sky,
Pale with the birth of day. That day, we said,
We will go seek the wilderness together —
And now she does not love me any more
Nor ever loved me save in one crazed hour.

> (*He looks at his watch again*)

Two minutes gone. But, oh, the years, the years!

> (*He walks restlessly about the room, stopping
> before the St. Michael hanging over his bed*)

Old boy, you could not root out all the dragons.
Time's one of them that lives.

> (*He goes to the door left again and listens*)

All's quiet there.

> (*He turns quickly and crosses the stage to the
> bureau, the top drawer of which he opens,
> throwing a quick glance over his shoulder as
> he does so. He picks up a revolver and some
> cartridges, opens the breach, and examines the
> weapon*)

I wonder — would she mind — even a little?

*(He loads the pistol slowly. One of the cart-
ridges sticks and he draws it out again, ex-
amines it, and throws it on the bureau. For
a moment he hesitates, sunk in thought)*

How empty always seemed the death of those
Who, all impatient, snatched from time the blade!
How void of compensation! for when God,
The never satiate, takes of Himself
Man's life, in truth some payment He will give
For the rude theft, but so, when man is thief
What can he hope to get, but at the best
A black, unpeopled, unresounding night?
Perhaps I should be born again to toil
In grayness more profound. The sweat - shop's
    noise,
The clangor of machines, the piteous wail
Of women bearing children in the slums
Of seething capitals, throbs in my ears,
Guessing perhaps what other births might bring.
And Lucy might despise me did I die,
Where now she only does not love, and God!
Her hate would burn in me a thousand years.

*(He lays the revolver on the bureau and looks
toward the door at the left, pensively)*

How strange that she can sleep, when yesterday
Those eyes of hers so waking and so wild

114

Seemed to cry out farewell to sleep forever.
Broughton! That after all it should be he!
And I was sure, so very, very sure
That I had won.

> (*There is a knock on the door*)

Blair

> (*In panic, thrusting the revolver into the
> drawer*)
>> Broughton! He knows, he knows!
> (*Then, standing with his back against the bu-
> reau, in a low voice that he tries in vain to
> steady*)

Come in!

> (*Broughton enters*)

Broughton
(With forced cheeriness)
Hello, Blair! Why, what's up? Your face
Looks like a lost soul's come in sight of Judgment.

Blair

That's just — my face.

Broughton
>> You scarce expected me?

I hardly thought you would. But you *will* keep
Such early hours —

Blair
(*Dully*)
What do you want of me?

Broughton
(*Nonchalantly, though his eyes are watching
Blair closely*)

Nothing but my umbrella that I left
Here if I'm not mistaken.

> (*Blair looks at him without answering, an ex-
> pression of question on his face, as though he
> doubted that reason for Broughton's return*)

> (*Broughton searches the corners for his umbrella,
> then goes to the bureau. Blair has turned
> toward the window, where he stands with
> his back to the audience. Broughton suddenly
> discovers the cartridge on the bureau and
> looks up at Blair sharply*)

Blair
(*Turning suddenly*)
Broughton!

Broughton
(*Quietly*)
                                        Well?
       Blair
The rain came after you were here. You know
You came with no umbrella.

              Broughton
              (*Nods*)
                        You are right.
          Blair
       (*Taken aback by his avowal*)
What do you want of me?

              Broughton
              (*Very seriously*)
                        I'm glad I came.
          Blair
Broughton, I'm not!

              Broughton
              (*With irony*)
                        So I should judge.
This cartridge here — defective, is it? Yes,
Bent at the rim, and so no candidate
For lord high executioner of cowards —
Tells well enough why you are sorry to see me.

117

Blair

Broughton, not that! If I were coward, I
Had sought my pay day with the gods long since.

Broughton

And what were then the wage that you had earned? —
Flinging your job down at the boss's feet
With "Take it back! I 'll none of it! I want
A million dollars and an ocean yacht,
A share in railroads and in politics,
A son with debts, a daughter who elopes,
A wife whose charities are manifold,
Dispensed to friends at terrapin and bridge.
All this I want, great God. Take back your clerk
And send me forth a prince or not at all."
Was that the thought?

Blair

(*Beginning quietly, but waxing excited as he goes on*)

                    No, that was not the thought.
You would not understand. Your soul is blent
Of other stuffs than mine. You see the world,
A rolling cask upon an infinite sea;
You pierce its vapors, and your eyes, like stars,
See all the universe, all — but themselves.
Men are to you massed as the Milky Way;
A hundred million as one sweep of light

Flash on your vision when your lips say : Man.
But I am one of those whose individual fire
You cannot see. For monstrous distances
Your telescope is set. You see an age
Reflected in the beggar's gaping wound,
But scarce the beggar's misery and pain.

> (*Blair stops and walks up and down the room,*
> *halting as before in front of the St. Michael*
> *hanging over the bed. Broughton, his bearded*
> *chin resting on his hand, is listening very in-*
> *tently*)

St. Michael here — he was like you. He crushed
A dragon, and they praise him still, in church.
But I like old St. Patrick better. Dragons
Have never plagued me half as much as snakes.
The little griefs are those that drive us mad. —
What do you know of human drudgery ?
The same walk to the subway every day,
The same gray streets, the biting shriek of the
       cars
Wheeling about the curve at Union Square,
The wan, tired faces and the same dun sights ;
And in the trains the heavy air, the crowds
Like cattle in a pen who graze by day
To eat and live, no more. You never sold
Your body and your brain for dollar bills !
I did. The price was small. I had to live.

I was the youngest, everybody's slave.
What did it matter that I had more brains?
The one who gets least pay is dog for all.
I ran their errands, cleaned their ink-wells for them,
Did what they ordered even when the clerks,
The very pettiest, bossed me like a nigger.
I did n't mind that, but the whole day long
I had to hear their whispered dirty talk,
And all the night I heard it in my sleep
And heard myself, myself repeating it;
Till it became like all the rest, a part
Of drudgery. Is this a human life?

Broughton

(*Quietly*)
An hour ago I might have pitied you.
But you had more than I had ever guessed.
Is Lucy dead?

Blair

(*Startled*)
    Lucy?

Broughton

      She loved you, Blair?
That were enough to make a heaven of hell!

Blair

Loved me, you say? Broughton, can *you* think that?

Broughton

Is it not true?

Blair

The bitterness of that lie
You of all men should know.

Broughton

(*Sternly now and insistently*)

Is it not true?

Blair

Why do you ask — that way?

Broughton

(*As above*)

Where's Lucy gone?

Blair

(*Drawing in his lips as he breathes heavily*)

Yes, the umbrella story *was* a lie.
You've come to pump me, come at dawn of
     day
When you knew well that I had care enough.

Broughton

You said that you were going away. I guessed
Your destination.

121

Blair

            Broughton, you were wrong.
The — pistol — was an impulse. You were wrong.
I 've bought — a ticket for Australia, and at five
I leave — this morning, so it 's just — good-by
Once more.

Broughton

        One ticket, Blair ? Just one ?

Blair

                        You thrust
Your knife in me, and turn and turn it round,
Cold-blooded, in the wound ! My life is mine
And I may live it how and where I please.

Broughton

There you mistake. Your life is not your own.
From birth to death your every slightest deed
Fetters with chains your individual fate
Forever with the fate of all mankind.
Sprague there, and Gallison, the pettiest clerk
Who nauseated you with dirty tales —
You 're linked to him ; the beggar on the street
Once you have looked on him is part of you.
The girl that stared at you from hollow eyes,
The shivering newsboy and the hungry, wan
Salvation Army woman with her kettle
Kept boiling for less hungry ones than she —

Are yoked beneath the same dark yoke as you
And harnessed to the same stiff chariot-pole.
Blair, do you hear? D'you think that you can go
To heaven's high hill or the devil's own retreat,
Heedless of — Lucy — of myself or Vane?
You're bound to us, bound head and heel and heart.

Blair

A merry chain-gang are we all!

Broughton
       Perhaps.
Call it a chain-gang or a brotherhood —
The fact remains — you cannot break the chain.
So, you'd escape? I was in Maine a month.
When I returned last night — some things — had
  changed.
I saw old Vane — I've known him twenty years,
And yet I scarcely recognized him now —
Half-crazed and bent with grief, with blood-shot eyes
And trembling limbs, grown aged in a week.
Vane always was a tyrant, but his love
For Lucy made him soft as any woman.
Her mother died when Lucy was scarce three.
So he was mother, father — all in one.

Blair
(*Softly, painfully*)
I did not know her mother died so young.

Vane told me all.

(*Then, gently laying his hand on Blair's shoulder*)

Blair, where is Lucy gone?

Blair

(*Quietly, half defiantly*)

She disappeared on Wednesday night.

Broughton

(*Looking steadily, sorrowfully in Blair's face*)

Come, Blair!
You know that that's no news. Where is she gone?

Blair

Why do you come to me?

Broughton

Late Wednesday night
You were at Vane's

Blair

Who said that?

Broughton

On our way
Uptown this morning Sprague, with that short laugh

He always sets as prologue to his tales,
Told me — what he called a good joke — on you.

Blair

You don't trust Sprague?

Broughton

                    He saw you climb the fence
Into Vane's yard. The basement door was open.
There was no light and so he saw no more.
He did not tell Vane what he saw. It seems
That there is honor even among thieves
Of women.

Blair

Broughton!

Broughton

                    It was wrong of Sprague
Not to tell Vane. No one suspected you.
Your good name stood up round you like a wall.
The boys said you were priggish, I'd have said
Merely that you were straight.

(*With a faint smile*)

                              I never thought
Of you as playing the Lothario.
I'd sooner feared a tumble for myself.
You were so bound up in your cotton-goods.

125

Blair

(*Speaking with difficulty, supporting himself
against the table*)

There, that's just it! Bound up! Why, I was
    wrapped
From head to heel with them. I saw the world
With eyes dimmed with a blind — of cotton-goods,
I heard, I spoke it seemed, through triple veils
Of — cotton-goods, and all the world span round
The price the world would pay — for cotton-goods.
You write your books and get your royalties.
Easy enough if you 've the gift. But who
Can live our drudge's life and not lose heart?
Like schoolboys damned through all eternity
To figure sums out of a printed book,
We spend our days with sales we have n't made
Of goods we 've never even known by sight.
That 's the clerk's life.

Broughton

        They paid you for your work.
You chose it of your own free will. No force
Pressed you into the service.

Blair

(*Bitterly*)

          Oh, they paid me.
But the Italian digging in the streets

Gets for his arm more than I for my brain.
When times were good and millions in and out
Passed through my books, d' ye think they gave me
      more,
That I might feel at least akin to them
Even though remote? No whit! And then last fall
In the great Panic, do you think they'd felt
They owed me something for the work of years?
They threw me out. I starved. You helped me then.
When things grew straight they took me in again.
I starved some more, that I could pay you back.

Broughton

I never knew it, Blair.

Blair

                    You never guessed.
'T was then that I met Lucy. You remember?
You took me there, but old Vane hedged her round.
Sundays we walked out in the Park together —
Not by appointment — she would not do that —
But then, I knew the places she loved best.
Oh, how the long days dragged till Sunday came!
Then I found true something you once had said,
" In life or death love is the saving grace."

Broughton

What love, what love?

Blair

                Some find it on the street —
So the clerks said — I never found it there.
I saw only the painted, hollow cheeks,
The bold hard eyes. My love was pure — at least
I thought that it was pure.

Broughton

                     Where is she gone?
Where have you taken her?

Blair

                   She was a drudge
As I was, working in a shop uptown,
Working as hard as I. She feared her father
She would not let me see her at her home.
But Wednesday night — I came

Broughton

                  Sprague told the truth?

Blair

(With a slow affirmative nod)

You said her father loved her? On that night
He beat her till she cried. She'd lost her job.
Vane was afraid he'd have to work himself.
Little you knew him Broughton. He had thoughts,

128

And nice ideas of human charity —
Vane's charity did not begin at home.
    (*Looking up suddenly*)
Vane had gone out. We scarcely spoke a word,
Lucy and I. We did n't need much speech.
She merely pinned her hat on; and we went
Silently out into the sultry night.
One thing she said : " If Broughton were but here.
Broughton has always helped me."

Broughton
(*With compressed lips*)
         She said that ?
I was away. I did not know her trouble.

Blair
A hundred things you wise men never know !

Broughton
Where is she now ? She 's here ?

Blair
(*Slowly*)
       Yes. — Let her sleep.
The storms will rise about her soon enough.
But we shall go away. Vane thinks her dead.
Let him still think it.

129

Broughton
(*Thoughtfully*)
And you married her —

That night?

Blair
(*After a long pause*)
We — did not — marry.

Broughton
(*Clutching Blair by the shoulders*)
Blair! By God
I did not know that I could hate you so,
Or feel the murder itching in my hands
As now I feel it. Like a kitchen wench
You took her, like a street-girl, like a slut,
Like a cigar to smoke and throw away,
A stump into the gutter! Were you glad
And happy in your conquest, did she please
        you?
Or are you ready to return her now
And boast to other girls how you had won her?

Blair
(*Seeking to free himself*)
Let go your hold! And judge me when you know!
We wanted life — life at its richest, best,
And most untrammeled, life in red and gold,

130

In fire and splendor, life at burning noon —
Even if we died for it. A suicide
Of opium-eaters dreaming glowing dreams
Before the end — perhaps 't was that. We sent
The twilight fugitive and knew the sun,
The burning, mortal sun — that was enough.
Men die for want of light — we two were glad
To die achieving it, and welcome death.
We drudges have our yearnings, even we,
For something from a better world than ours.
Priests call it God, you wise men call it Beauty.
I do not know. We cried for something big,
Rising titanic, unresigned, unbowed,
Out of a world of crawling pettiness —
Sin! If you will. Triumph it was to us
And liberty from man — and God!

Broughton
(*With hands behind his back has walked in
an attitude of the deepest misery toward the
window, where he turns and speaks, smiling
wanly, bitterly*)

                              Sin? Blair,
Was that the beauty that you sought, was that
The paint to tinge the drudgery, the grayness?
(*He goes to the window*)
Look at the city, at the empty streets
So shiny with the rain, the misty lights

Like captured fireflies — Blair, what do you see?
Beauty? It's there. You call it ugliness.
You, too, are right, for over all, you see
A sickly shadow, drooping like the night
Over a plague-touched town, full of mad forms —
Because men deem relief from drudgery
Waits on the rolling Juggernaut of sin.
Look at the houses, wretched, dark, unclean,
Sombre with misery and discontent.
Why, why? You know it in your heart!
It's this mad striving after phantom lights
That seem to promise refuge on the marsh,
But lure us all the deeper into quicksands.
Beauty too tangible is cheap and vain
And liberty from God and man is bondage.

Blair

A phrase! A pretty phrase! Fit for a man
Who thinks in terms of stars and never sees
The single aching heart. Perhaps in dreams
Your world is true, in life it's one for one.
And only we who dare to mock your laws
Can from the dust-heap pick our gem — and live.

Broughton
(Painfully)

The dust-heap? Did you mean that, Blair? Did she —
Know she was groping — in a heap — of dirt?

Blair
(*Agonized*)
Broughton! You turn things so. God knows I tried
To make her happy.

Broughton
      Blair, had I but known
How drudgery was eating at her heart!

Blair
(*Ironically*)
You did not know.

Broughton
      She had a happy strain.
She sang to me, and seemed so light of heart —
How should I guess?

Blair
(*To himself bitterly*)
      To me she never sang. —

Broughton
Had I guessed!
    (*Suddenly grasping Blair's arm and looking him
    full in the face*)
      Blair, what do *you* know of love?
133

Blair

(*Slowly, as he realizes the whole meaning of Broughton's words*)

You — love — her ? — Broughton, it 's not true !

Broughton

(*Simply*)

Not true ?

Why should I now deny it ? She has chosen
After her will. I long gave up my right
To gain love for myself. I 'm growing old.
Forty is old — for some men. And I 'm gray.
She could not love me.

Blair

Broughton, stop ! Your voice
Makes me a coward.

Broughton

Love her, love her, Blair !
Love her a thousand times, and love her more !
It 's not the love we get that makes our hea-
        ven,
The love we steal chasing with hungry heart
The fruits of love. It 's what we dumbly give
That builds a world,
A shimmer as of sunrise on the streets,
An aureole as a saint's about men's heads.

134

It's love, that flows from one to the wide world —
A poor, dumb world, too feeble to respond.

Blair

Love for a world, love for a world! Blind talk!
You sat up on your pinnacle of dreams
And never saw us!

Broughton

     Blair, enough of this.
We cannot heal the past. The future holds
Its own pure, rounded life if we but claim it.
Come, call her, Blair. When she was small, she loved
To go to me and let me soothe her pains.
It may be I can ease them even now.

Blair
(Bitterly)

So I must call her, let you dry the tears
That I have caused to flow? That were true justice
On me, but God! I'll not yet give her up!

Broughton

There is no thought of that.

Blair

       So *you* may say.
But she is mine, she's all I ever had,
She's mother, father, money, health, and fame,

135

All that I longed to be and never was,
Bound all in one. Even though she hate me still
There's always hope that some day she may love.

Broughton

Hate you?

Blair

You never knew the best of life,
So you 'll scarce miss it, not, at least, as I
Who knew it for an hour — or for a day.
Go, Broughton, you 've been good to me. Don't
    change
The good to ashes now. For your own peace,
Broughton, go now, and let us find our way —
Lucy and I — alone. For your own peace! —

Broughton

For my own peace? Why do you speak of me?

Blair

It 's nothing. Only go!

Broughton

No! Blair, you spoke
Of hate.

Blair

Mere words. Broughton, it 's our own lives
We have to live. Don't snare your better fate

136

With ours. There's only sorrow as reward —
Sorrow for — Lucy — and for you and me.

Broughton

I'll know it!

Blair

No.

Broughton

(*Coming close to Blair, with unwavering persistence*)

I'll take the fate that comes.
My mill is strong. 'T will grind it.

Blair

Are you sure?

Broughton

The rack is worse than hanging. Tell it, Blair.

Blair

Last night we quarreled.

Broughton

You and Lucy? Blair!

Blair

'T was scarce a quarrel. But a curtain fell
Thick as a storm between us. 'T was my fault.
I thought that she had loved me. — I was wrong.

My God, Blair, and she told you that?

Blair

Still more.
Her love for me was as a rocket's flare —
A burst of stars — the stick falls in the lake —
So lustreless and common once 't is quenched.

Broughton
That was not Lucy!

Blair

No, it was a drudge
Burdened with loneliness, mad with regret.

Broughton
Lucy?

Blair

She loved — another, and the love
Burnt like a flame unnoticed, burnt and grew
Into consuming fire. You never guessed —

Broughton
(*Mechanically*)
I — never — guessed.

Blair
The man she loved —

138

Broughton

Don't say it, Blair! My God!

Blair

The man she loved —

Broughton

(*Grasping Blair, who has turned toward the
door at the left, roughly by the shoulders*)

Say it!

Blair

Was you!

Broughton

Blair — Blair!

Blair

(*His hand on the door-knob*)

Now are you satisfied, now you have all?

(*Blair throws open the door and leaps back,
overcome by the fumes of gas that stream
from the inner room. Broughton gives a cry*)

Broughton

The gas, the gas!

(*He darts to the door, but Blair pushes him
roughly aside and enters. His cry of horror
is heard, followed by the sound of breaking
glass as he smashes the windows. A second*

139

later he stumbles out of the room, strangling,
and falls into the arms of Broughton, who
draws him to the open window)

Blair
(Gasping, and clutching Broughton's arms)
Dead, Broughton, dead! Her face
Swollen and livid. Dead for hours — dead — dead —

Broughton
(In agony, trying to free himself)
Blair — let me go — to her.

Blair
(Choking)
No — she is mine.
(He rises slowly and moves toward the door
again, clasping Broughton's hand with the
pressure of complete understanding)
Broughton, the saving grace, the saving grace.
(He goes unsteadily to the door, halts at the
threshold an instant, with a tightening of the
muscles, then passes out. Broughton, standing
with his back to the window, follows him
with his eyes in which there gleams a look
of hopeless agony. Outside, the clock in the
church steeple slowly and sonorously strikes

five. A single ray of sunlight falls through the window on the left wall. Broughton draws himself together, his strength and his faith seem to come back to him).

Blair

(Reappears at door left, gasping for breath. He points with a faint smile at the patch of sunlight on the floor)

The sunlight!

Broughton

(Mechanically going forward and turning out the gas still burning from the jet over the table)

Yes, it's day now.

CURTAIN

The Riverside Press

CAMBRIDGE . MASSACHUSETTS

U . S . A